Epiphanies on tl

Epiphanies on the Promenade

Selected Poems

Robert Prochaska

Iliad Press
Chicago

Copyright 2004 by Robert Prochaska

All rights reserved. Except for review passages, this book may not be reproduced in whole or in part, or in any form without permission from the publisher.

Some of these poems have appeared previously in the following publications: "The City," *Slipstream* (1983); "Sentiments From a Used Car Lot in Jersey," *The Passaic Review* (1983); "Training Models," *Exquisite Corpse* (1986); "Mass Murderer," "A Telephone Call Made in an Attempt to Stir Communication," *The Louisville Review* (1987/1988); "Christmas Eve, 1981," *Pipe Dream* (1982); "A Letter From Iowa," *Woodrose* (1983); "Pigeons of 50th St." "Nights Gone By," *AW* (1984); "Laying There," "Torment," "Black Glove Madam in Vegas," "Willow," "A Known Anonymity," "Reunion," "Impression," "To Here & Back (To Jack Kerouac)," *Fourfront*, Bearstone Publishing: Farley, Iowa, 1982.

Manufactured in the United States.
First edition.

Iliad Press
P.O. Box 1202
Chicago, Illinois 60017-1202

Library of Congress Control Number: 2003111169

ISBN 0-9625306-3-8

Epiphanies on the Promenade

Of Embryos and Moons

Prologue

They came from barren country
to find loam and river valley coal,
to wander as raven and storm
across the lantern's merciful light.

Marriage before first plowing,
cathedral bells swelling to the undulations
of sacred earth,
entreaties spoken in rooms
where memory fuses with youth.

A parlor is dusty, silent, filled with mothballs.
Farmers traverse heaven with their eyes.

I.

My, what honored pretty ones!
What do you know of love?
An owl's hair, black against the windowpane,
a baby in pink attentiveness
but distracted by marigolds and daisies.
The woodshed merging with tender heat,
a prairie raw and earth-burning.

America will laugh at Paris,
literature, the known world.

II.

Woodrow Wilson orders bonds for the inebriated,
future harvests freeze on railroad tracks
as icy eaves collapse
upon thin walls of consciousness.

Mary holds an empty milk bottle
to her chalky lips, pines to understand
her mercenary sister, born on Christmas Day.
Father refuses to hear the crying,
his heels dug into the floor,
whiskey bottle tight around his mouth.

III.

It's a perplexing void, Kansas a dustbowl,
long lines for soup on Shepherd's Row,
East Broadway, West Broadway,
perimeters of death.

"We will do what is best for America," ring the voices
of politicos from radios insensate.
"We will make the world over for reform,"
promise the evangelists.

Father snores.
A torch for a lip for a song.
Detroit is crafting engines, chassis, and wheel
but nothing moves the soul.
The mercenary daughter is small enough
to fit into a cigar box.

IV.

Men worry, their money in vaults,
frustrations in the mind
fulminating against the growing madness.
Scotty in Babylon,
Papa in the trenches.

It had to be you.
It had to be you, Mister!
No one could pass you by.
Dump your handsome sons to war.
Dump your ugly ones too.
War, you take the finest fabric of men,
wipe them off on your sleeves,
written epitaphs.

V.

Item: A Slavic man, disinherited,
moving from town to town,
meets the mercenary daughter
in one of his speakeasies,
is introduced by his brother
takes her for cocktails to propose
a honeymoon on the crap tables,
furs flung over her shoulders
crystal chandelier oblivion.

Married, he hangs his Army uniform
in the attic, to grow up with the bats.

VI.

Fruit preserves in the summer kitchen.
A brown patch of lawn where tobacco lay
spat from the porch.
Tears in grandfather's delicate dysfunctioning eyes,
torn from that dream of two arms
once coiled around his neck.
A vision of Mary, her little sister in the crib,
the day she put on lipstick and walked out the door.

Boys play touch football under dirty arc lights,
glommed by fishflies bred from the river.
Mercenary, now mother, clutches her vulva in horror
and runs from the bedroom where the youngest coos.

VII.

In the aftermath of dames and booze
a father becomes insolent, surrenders to machine-like motions
and the passing of days.
Three women run to his bedside,
past town gossips, to their mother
who clings to him, corncob pipe by his side.

The river is saintly, affirms the lifeline
of hominids, manservants,
even the bloodless yet to come.
Ghosts trample trees, and maple leaves
fall in hazy distances
where the world is composed of brave, brave men.

Part One

451 Sherwood

Dirt and acorns.
Grass and sky.
Boys and whiskey.
Hate and rye.
Girls would turn into women,
and their every word would be connected to earth
in a way no man could imagine.

At one absolute moment in a stunningly dull world,
the green-and-yellow Caterpillar tore up the dirt field
on the corner facing the river,
field of our greatest games and strategies,
our most daring headfirst catches.
The dirt stayed in a heap overnight,
its primordial essence a milky loam.
Those girls were crying now for sure
knowing what they had just glimpsed father do,
how brutally his hand came down.

At 8 a.m. the workmen were back
hauling the tempestuous past away.
Grandpa cupped his pipe on red leather
as the new road was dragged, tarred, and rolled.
The plump faces of neighbor women
ever-so-gently brushed aside the curtains.
I took a baseball and felt the seams, over and over,
till I turned the world on its dreary head.
Sleep was the healer.
Eisenhower came back to the Big House,
and another 4,000 babies were brought into God's garden.

Going To The Cemetery, Ten Years Old

Ambushed in a car on Memorial Day
by family and friends, to lay flowers on Uncle John's grave,
I came to learn the urgency of kind words
that otherwise fill a vacuum
in turbulent weather
and to contemplate the lap of luxury
its useless limousines that ride in space
in magazine ads
while here at the stone marker, a human being
who needed nothing more than a decent woman
and a laugh at the bar,
came from Czechoslovakia to Iowa
to be by my feet
and my mother's old, old paisley dress
she wore for such occasions
as make her get to her knees –
and when I came in from the warm air
to a shower of light that milked the heavy drapes
I dropped into dronish calm on the sofa,
convinced the world would not harm me
nor give my anything I didn't earn.

Uncle Reuben

When Uncle Reuben came to your door
with corn from the 40 acres,
families shrieked in anticipation
of the buttered delights to be served
and crows rested in niches of pine trees
below the valley.
Mothers bought photo albums
and patted their babies in the womb
while cleats clopped on paved roads
where neighborhood jocks talked of the future
and the promise of fatherhood
lurked in their dreams.

Only a few people saw Reuben on his rounds,
for he moved swiftly and rarely emerged from home,
built partially underground over a ditch
of thistles and thorns.
Reuben's wife stayed on the 40 acres
to admire his handiwork, left only to go to flea markets
in a straw hat that fell over her face
and prevented you from hearing what she had to say.

The day Reuben died, on a day near
the ceremony of the corn,
no one paid much attention
to the broken-backed way people walked,
nor to Reuben's wife,
who reluctantly went underground
to live out her years in awe of the 40 acres.

Invoking a Higher Authority

I.

The church altar on a late Saturday afternoon
in spring, always my best night.
I knew no one would be there, dinnertime was near,
families not quite ready for relaxation.
The watery aroma of chrysanthemums gripped my nostrils
as I entered the vestibule.
I could taste the lilies and dream of faraway ports
in the stained glass, the dull warmth of the day
muted
in purple capes and flowing robes.

II.

Saturday evening in spring,
near normal temperature, alone in my house.
I prepared my own altar, complete with white cloth
and chalice (a covered plastic cup).
Playing servant and martyr, miscreant and saint.
Only I could foresee the pallor of night,
the way fog beat down my street
a baseball game on the transistor, semi-tragic
from Comiskey Park.
All the gods had a name,
except one that peered at me from the yard,
shifting in the damp leaves.

Utensil

There was promise to the evening,
the new LIFE magazine to read,
a house snug in winter, the land we lived in
protected and free.
Newspapers stirred little dissent.
Soda had no taste and school no memory.

Then halfway through dinner
he ranted from the evil drink
and mother cried in a swollen heap.
The tine of the fork from my brother's rage
descended into father's meaty hand, sinking into
the shrieks and mayhem.

But a little boy has to go to sleep.
Forsake the dream, for it is too powerful.
Become anything you want to be.
A utensil, a particle of food,
the hum of the kitchen clock.

Used Bed

A leather baseball glove snaps an imaginary ball
into its spit-slicked pocket.
Pennants hang by a piece of old tape.
Wallpaper comes off in odd places.
Snores mingle with the dead.
Stars drip light onto ebony grass.
Sour apples fall from lapping leaves
as I burden myself
with what I missed a million other nights.

Unmailed Letter

I wanted to rampage you,
a wounded Oedipalite whose visions
filled nights with Circe, Hippolyta,
and nymphs with no genitalia.
I'm a man now and I think it bothers you
to relinquish your men,
even as you resolved to stay by your husband
as he invoked his private obscenities.

It is a mechanized age with fewer mothers,
and we do seem out of touch
like live wires teasing each other.
If I was a prisoner it was only because
you tried to make of me a criminal
for resisting your charms.

Tomboy

We took five rolls of blue and pink
toilet paper, and wrapped them
around the house
while the ex-Marine was inside
reading TIME, and his daughter,
hoping for some end to this dalliance,
crawled into my '63 Impala.

We found a vacant garage
behind a doctor's house
where we took turns
with her hair, eyes,
and thighs
the stars graciously lit.

Virgin

We wanta send the old man to Vegas.
Showgirls won't dazzle him, not at 77.
That's right, 7 and 7.
An old bootlegger who dodged the limelight.
Blushed at strippers who bent down to kiss him.

Send the old man to Vegas.
Wastelands have no Venus.
Who cares if it's Newton or Sinatra?
It's all palpable nonsense for the old man.
Send him right away.
Get him to the blackjack tables,
that's what he has in mind.
Don't let him stir or sit too long
or offend him by placing his bet.

I guarantee we all die too soon.
To hell with images and false assurances.
Roll the die.
Send the old man to Vegas.
Give him the lights and candy strippers
but don't leave him out in the sun.
You know, his white skin and ultraviolet.
I'll call you 10-to-1 he'll snicker and swim
grasp straws in the hazy desert air.
He'll realize his biggest bets were all before him,
that objects aren't as dear as they used to be,
they're just there.

Send him to the airstrip,
westward ho,
give the old man Vegas
and let him glow.

Hilda

Quintessential mother of the quilt-and-sew set.
Dr. Spock's Secretary of State.
A martini baby from GI Joe's hash dreams,
voluptuous hair woven from Freud's classic mien,
a stern apparition
confronting the blossoming woman-beast.

Even on the telephone with her girlfriend
the metallic chatter is catharsis.
She loved Kennedy and pot roast,
and Nat King Cole on the record player
as she lay with her thighs showing
in monophonic wonderment.

Sparrows

Sparrows make me stop
and elate
in the wonders of a heart,
tied to bone,
and the tiny eyes of change
that need to see only
what is
what is
and to favor no man over another.
Only sparrows do this for me.

Ritual

We eat in this cluster of indifference
after fighting about which restaurant we'll use,
understanding that all restaurants here
serve goliath potatoes and thick steaks
with full bottles of Heinz ketchup and Lazy Susans
that always have too many carrots, and that my little niece
will spill something to get her father mad and lead
to an argument that will lead to a angry renunciation
of something always disagreed with anyway,
and when our mother fails to hear the casual remark
another argument ensues which will make my niece
do something brave like throw a cherry from dessert
onto her father's lap, and again he'll turn red and we will be led
into an argument that already has been unresolved
and then we will pay the bill, stare at each other
and wonder what diseases each of us will obtain
as we grow old among and away from each other,
because of each other and despite each other, and then
we will go home and try to be civil though a few arguments
here and there, splinter ones from the time of the cherry-throw,
will erupt, and then I pack my suitcase, get in the car,
and meet the old walrus-like guy I used to talk baseball with,
and we'll talk baseball at the airport, and then I'll get on the
plane, watch my father and mother argue again, get off the plane
and take a taxi going west on the LIE to Queens,
throw myself on my bed, and dream.

Elegant Faces

For all his chicanery, he glowed for her
in a dimly-lit nightclub.
She was duly impressed with his suit,
the way he smiled, the things she had to say
to get him hooked.
Married, she turned into a swan,
bought him a set of golf clubs he used once,
in 1949.

It's easy to see the trains slow crawl east
from my hill overlooking the Mississippi.
Occasionally a freighter stops
and smoke billows out of the high trees
for the sake of a glum son like me.

His Army jacket, starched into cement,
was hung in its sacred place,
next to the owl on the windowsill
who grieves for no one.

Evolution of A Marriage

You baited her in a steamy Chicago nightclub
with one of the Dorseys playing.
Her hands made for holding,
her hair made for hands,
she sought much beyond the tin roof home.
Her Daddy drank, like you only more.
An entrepreneur, always in demand,
you had no dread of bills.

Beast met child/beauty and scored.
In the photo your eyes are lit with the fuse of youth,
and later that evening
(that went largely unrecorded)
you had a chance to get a shot
at those long, long legs,
well proportioned,
and smiled to think of her father
swigging it down good, as you were
in your own way.

They say disease catches up with man,
anger and remorse too.
They say the naked eye
will sometimes reject the truth.
But I cannot sit idly by to be persuaded
that love's intensity dies.
Lately, those once-a-year hugs
have felt very good, father.
Legs and drinks and Dorseys die, so:
How about a hug, a hug for your son?

Hiya Pal

Was there any drink
Jack Dempsey wouldn't have his bartenders mix?
Tell me that story again, Dad,
the one about his long strides down Broadway.
Dempsey would say "Hiya pal."
Would Dempsey save the world
by saying "Hiya pal" to the men
in the Defense Department?
Nobody in war wants to be pals.

The old champ won't be there
when filling stations in the Nevada desert
are rusty oil cans and faded Zephyr lettering
in a sandstorm.
But I'll write something sad, champ,
to make it feel like you're walking
across this land,
a man wounded
a man profaned.

Mother

So many times without fail you'd ask some inanity,
question some trivial point,
while my brain gyrated with grave import.
I huddled by the furnace duct in winter,
crunching my body up into a ball
hoping to resuscitate spring.
The mornings opened up with a rigidity,
as if all had been done but still must be completed.
The same Presidents, the same car wrecks,
the same ballplayers breaking your heart come October.

Your undying love for your husband,
who never left his deserters, nor forsook his enemies,
was noble.
I remember he swore under his breath,
in unison with you,
whenever I sat to furiously scribble words
(Look, he thinks he's a writer!)

Mother, I am so much sadder because of you,
for I'm the blond-haired boy on your front porch
who brings back the frontier of September,
when fire consumed the trees.

Self-Examination During a Tornado

To the basement I ran where the smell of urine
was buried in the drainage system
by the southwest corner where I was told to go
in case of high winds, and large spiders
skittered from cobweb to cobweb.
Here I surmised no demon could reach me,
I'd work the punching bag
until the sky went from purple to black.
No one could take me back.
White heat opened my lungs
and a void in the universe appeared
where Ariel flew, and scattered telephone poles
and trees across the landscape.

After it was over I was relieved humanity was alive,
that a rainbow fell over grazing cattle
on the far hill,
and red blips on the radio tower
restored our measured breathing.

Black Glove Madam in Vegas

Her sister probably died on the Salt Flats
whistling a happy tune.
There she was, at the bottom of the desert,
pulling on metal erections
to get a silver touch of coin
that does not penetrate skin,
or anything.
Sad, soiled glove
worn through to neon bones,
obliterated by my tears.

The highway was boiling.
No one said to leave.
I trained my eyes on the jackrabbit
that wasn't there.

Spinning Tunes In the Back

On a bad day
I walked into the No Name Bar,
hugged the jukebox
and went directly to Buddy Holly.
The drink was alive,
I was alive,
and that smooth guitar
took the bullshit out of every crooked mouth.

Traveling Salesman

My brother is a salesman,
drives around Iowa in a company car,
listens to favorite rock 'n roll songs
or just fidgets with the pained faces
walking to the unemployment line.
He turns the bend that goes around
the emptied factories of Davenport
as the black children of nowhere disappear
with a rubber ball
down an alleyway where their fathers
and father's fathers set up house.

My brother gets out of the car,
sweating, feeling like the human race
has been misused, this distinct knowledge
comes out in rage, sometimes distraction.
He's white and he knows he's in a strange area.
He tries to raise his daughters, do the business at hand,
finish it off, get back on the road.
A few neons are on along the seven o'clock showdown
Friday night, when the finery comes out
and the cow towns go asleep in the plane of lights
called the Quad Cities.

There goes that rage inside, but now he tunes in
Smokey Robinson over the car radio,
holds onto the steering wheel like he held on
nights when the sirens bent his ears in Nam.
You see, my brother's a salesman,
drives around Iowa in a company car.

Middleweight

My bacon and eggs were snapping in the pan
as I eyed the man with a scar under his jaw
running to his cauliflower ear.
I don't look long on a man like that,
Irish, on the edge of poor,
still believing the morning news
will tell him something he doesn't know.

The rain of glass shards
struck a pool of black
and someone poked the hairy man
frying my eggs and said:
"That was Walter Wood, that guy right there,
was sitting right there?
Best left hand in the business,
fought Rocky Graziano."
Then I realized none of us lives long enough
for our own blood to catch up.

To Father, On the Night of Our Coming

I.

I wondered what it was like to breathe the dawn,
aching for food, alcohol swilling in your stomach,
a welter of sweat from bloodstream traumas
and the ghosts of bacteria blotching your hands.
I wondered if you would answer the dead-of-night
rings, as you moved in netherworlds of lost children
one gone by loss of favor
one by death.

I wondered if the silence would tell me anything
before I had to run back to bed,
one dead, loss of favor,
one through medical death, the second son,
as I am now the second son.
I wondered if all the money was worth it
if all the booze was worth it
if all the graduations were worth it
and drifted back to the time when you summoned us
to the grassy bank, to watch a wounded dove hop
into the air, crashing to the ground
as we tried to catch this illusion
before it escaped, into earth or sky
we still don't know.

II.

Out of a night alone
in the cool of alone, I detect the pungent odor
of burning wood in a rainy world
where a few humans cover their faces
from the fumes.
I will not be consumed, father,
not tonight, though this fire rages near,
dreaming of what's been lost is your game,
not mine.

Once you let it go, you let the devil claim you
and you were alive inside
but you preferred, somewhere down the line,
not to talk about it again.
Love is not lost on the dead
though the living be lost.
You tortured yourself trying to change that.
Yet in the lost winds of cool aloneness
of a night alone
I hold you, kiss you, sleep with you,
surround you with life
as sure as death turns beside you.

Interstate 80

The tiny demarcations between death and life
chase us every day, in the shadows,
like the time I fell 50 feet
landing perfectly between a dock and a boat's hull,
or the time a car sped by me within an inch of my body.
Always the urgency of a night's sleep
in a hotel bed too big for dreaming.
I violated the cardinal rule: I lived.
The corollary rule: You proceeded your dead brother,
and must by rights be alive for all to see.

My father lay centrally in this division
between life and what I thought might be my death.
I saw it one night in a hotel room in Chicago,
rain coming down in torrents on the mirror, on his face.
The last glimpse of him shaving, his charcoal face
omnipresent, the dark edges of disease.
His saving graces were his sons, his walls.
As the bus depot groaned, factory workers spread tales of woe
in the Rockford café that looked like old America.
The luncheonette girl stood in a patina of dusk,
while mother and father wavered
side by side on the crimson road.

Willow

Under the willow a boy was killed
by an errant shotgun blast.
In mythological quandary
his father's feet would paw the ground
where the echo wandered.
Usually a screen door would shut
and charge the air, grab you in stormclouds
occluding the earth, turn young eyes away
to the safety of their mother's porches,
where they could watch each thunderclap.

In the sun the strands swayed
and tried to heave each child who passed under
into its kaleidoscopic circus of colors.
Today, years after the wound
became the path home
became the womb,
a bucket of roses sits on a tree stump
where once the whisper of a willow
stirred the cool night.

A Widow's Timing in Spring

She's out there
trying to make it go right,
bending one knee to the moist earth
planting a single bud, her dress blowing fast
to the plane of her garden, black sky foreboding
and dead snakes inside forgotten brush.

She was tempted, at 50 degrees,
to let nature take over the leaf,
the goddess,
remembering Al and his shyness
the warm glow of war
written on his slender figure.
How handsome in uniform, creased and shaven!

A piece of snow from some ungodly region
strikes her nose, she is forced to inhale it.
Air chilling rapidly now, bearing in on brain.
Al would have known this was not the day
to plant, to test the rages March can bring.
It was a day to sit and read the papers
let the final howls of winter die.
Al would have surrendered, like he always did.
She gets up, stiffly, after one last look at the ground.

Summer In a Small Town

The movie theaters are filled.
I drive the town, possessed.

All those eyes in the dark,
won't let one secret
out.

A Known Anonymity

He called on me during one of his nameless,
numbing sleeps.
He had knocked on the door
scratched by three different dogs
over 30 years.
Mother duly answered.
She said he needed help,
that a part of his brain tissue
had been waylaid.
He used to be a fullback.
Ran like the wind in autumn
on solemn evenings
when I fumbled in my pants.

Reunion

I took the car I had driven
seven summers before,
took it over the Iowa bridge
at the end of the decade.
Full moon moving with the bridge,
cutting through the hills and trees,
dead center over neighbor Kennedy's white shingle house
with the basketball hoop in the driveway—
his log-cutting tools and instruments of the unknown
hanging inside the garage, where I threw
many an errant football pass
through the only window on the side.
Now it appears the size of a keyhole.

My father puts a coat over his pajamas
and we cut through the icy loneliness
of bridges, once more.
I think about the hollowness of birth.

To Here and Back (for Jack Kerouac)

There are too many sins to think of, Jack.
The are roads and enlightenment still.
The rainbow cleric exists.
So too shrouds,
one of which I discovered in Prospect Park
while confronting Jackie Robinson
stealing home.

I wound myself and wound others.
I ask why love, as you did.
To vibrate is dangerous and deceptive.
(Need I tell you?)
And always, Jack, always,
there is somewhere a muscle singing
and somewhere,
a man walking fast and thinking hard.

Traveling Poem

We edge toward dawn.
Greyhound trailing incinerator sadness.
Only four hours ago a sliver of moon
passed Pennsylvania,
lost Indians,
the sins of America.
I point homeward,
I point strong,
I never really thought I'd live this long.

We edge toward dawn.
So many sleeping, so many dreaming,
so many dead and in the ground.

Impressions

There is mud in the pure prairie sky,
the taste of blood
that tries to rise out of us
but is quartered in the bile of our passion.

It makes us too weak, spring,
and its angelic trees.
Climbing the cord of words
man is indissoluble,
a monarch butterfly on the tip of a bud.

What our eyes seize
is the wantonness in beasts,
their slow pulsations
in the fields beyond our breaths.

Template

It was a canary, that's all I knew,
and the grass was burned brown in August,
the old man's garden spurting a last few tomatoes
as I gulped from a water hose
in the late afternoon crystalline sadness,
the great aphrodisiac earth
conjoining his wings to the roots
that ran under the white picket fence
and separated lands from their rightful owners.

Now it is August again,
and a thousand miles away
that picket fence beckons,
and the canary we put in the White Owl cigar box,
snow now dust now sun.
If I put my head to the fire
I can hear the bird singing.

The Uncovered Man

Sweet contagion overtook my young bones
during 3 a.m. drives across the bridge,
back from her mobile home park.
The pungent autumn air clipped my cheeks
and the last few fireflies drifted to the riverbed.
She didn't need a man as much as an idea,
a budding writer impressed by female anatomy.
After we decided to break it off I saw her in a bar
in a tangle of light that echoed one thought:
her legs wrapped tightly around mine.

Too many times we liquored the night,
bringing with it no contentment come morning.
In that drive across the bridge there was a measure
of a man looking inward, wanting to reach farther,
but not knowing how.
The Mississippi mud was oozing up from the bottom,
as it always does when the tide is in.

The Process

All men must be saints.
All towns must be inhabited, or else uprooted.
All highways must be driven
or presented as gifts to the forlorn.
All elements must be evenly distributed,
or we are chemically malformed.
Sleep, dear father, we said what we had to.
You told me Uncle John put a severed thumb
inside a matchbox, kept it hidden
after the Quaker Oats factory exploded.
That day, you thought
you had played a joke on America.

Collision

He ran toward second base
where I had been hit by the runner,
nailed upright while watching the ball
tuck itself into the past.
I regained consciousness
with the smell of his cologne,
a whiff of powder under his hatband.
Shirt undone at the collar,
he appeared a lobsterman
who got lost in the middle of America.
But it was his boy, his creation,
who went down with the setting sun,
and though I don't remember his words
we became a newsreel of figures
that got up and went on.

The Summer League

There were hardened coaches
who taught me the morals of their fathers,
pegged me for the minor leagues.
They rearranged my batting stance,
hit ground balls to my left side.
There were young football players
who thought their sport had more guts,
brought their girls to watch,
knowing the ineffably sad shadows
falling in right field
would give them pause to wonder.

On deck, I faked disaffection with the game,
spread resin on the bat, pretended to scowl
and hear the game's rough edges, late-inning heroics.
I only fitfully displayed a hitter's savvy,
cracking a line drive over second base.

On the final day I played, at an hour
when fragrant suns kiss fair-haired boys into manhood,
the gap-toothed girl, always a part of my legend,
blushed and bowed.

Hootowl

A hootowl stared through my father's brains.
He perched like overnight baggage,
chronicling the moment.
A thousand dollars lay wet on the floor,
LOOK magazine on the mahogany bureau,
pictures that would never again
regain their rightful image.
The hootowl blinked twice a night
rendered time meaningless
in the deceptions of a half-moon.
Maybe a flying machine would land on our bones,
but the hootowl would not move.
While money crawled on all fours,
my father deep into a snore,
a furry beast showed his yellow eyes
like blood shot out of a birthstone.

Mississippi

The Mississippi
runs over
the unambitious young
spelling its dangers.
Holy battlements of factories
lay waste to beaches
and waters turn
into menacing gum
stretching
aching
blacking out
doubt.
Yet what fatigues the brain
is the dullness of sense.
Witness then
three boys
with pants rolled up
past their kneecaps
basking in the wild purity
of what they know
the dangerous
unambitious
Mississippi.

Cardinal

Nothing as pure as the Illinois cardinal
in a thicket of fresh fallen snow,
peeking from a dark-green hedge.
The onslaught of a fierce winter
should have kept him away.
But he showed his red crown and royal crest
through the white blast
when I was a young boy, and feeling depressed.
As the years hurtle onward I recall that bird,
and its faith in trees.
His blood roams among us,
and summons us from our burdens,
from our fractious hearts
that only crave loyalty.

A Letter From Iowa

We wait, like archangels for a happy hosanna,
as the whiplash snowstorm
George said would descend to take his eyes out
speeds down the street
to the little cove of warmth
he keeps
in Iowa.

We must find a shelter
with some measure of peace
and make a bucket of our brains
for the bed to hold—
humanity screams for a parcel of fear
a dedicated lover.

Seems we look forever
for some sign of nasty weather,
don't we, George?
Work, cars, landlords
don't ruffle us at times like these.
Clear-headed, typhoid ghosts
shout at us to hold watch.
I keep my elbows to the bench,
stay away from the sky.

Gazebo

She was a virgin
who danced inside the gazebo
on cool summer nights
when the table was set.
While sipping wine we would watch her
ruffle her lacy white dress,
wait for summer to turn
to give her womanhood.

And she was thighs
and mouth
and hair
black, black hair,
deviltry in motion
and with her went summer
and my illusions about the primacy of love
as it lifted above my drunkenness
and left the wind, alone,
inside the gazebo.

Curt

In his own backyard they found him,
muzzle in his mouth, veins of leaves
fitting into his self-same tissue
locked into tree limbs
his crossed eyes.
Down the hill a red-headed kid pumped gas,
working Curt's shift as a favor.
The rain had pressed his remaining flesh
deeper into a ravine of dying sunflowers.

By November the football stadium's harsh arc lamps
beat down upon checkered shirts and blankets.
A new moon blossomed out of the old.
In time, the body found,
men and women went to work differently,
and the red-headed kid, remembering Curt's face,
wiped tears behind thick windshields
where men constantly decide
whether to stay where they are
or travel onward.

Crickets In Pasture

My brother called from Clear Lake,
said they were still drinking to Buddy Holly,
that someone was found in a field
trying to find scraps of an engine.
It is wondrous to try to recoup lost immersions
in faith, as if we traveled roads too long
for our imagination.
Even a bloodied chicken will suffice,
or a bent penny.
How innocent the eyes when rapt
when human figures disappear behind trees
we don't bother to follow in the wind.

Buddy's twang and thump was enough to set us off,
ripping up the hall that night
in the dying snow,
the hell with the rock, the hell with the roll.
What can a boy do whose home is far away
but walk out into the cold air
and run into nowhere, screaming
"I got it, I got it!"

Wool Shirts

When stars steadied the October wind
and leaves frowned upon the glowering,
possessive earth,
my father would beat around the house
in his fine wool shirts,
stretching his body like the king lion he was.
All the homes had one light on
and I never imagined any other father
wearing heavy wool like my father,
or any other father who could jaunt around like mine,
inspecting the wind as it whipped around the brick
(and nobody moved).
A branch would snap
and I would drop my baseball
with the dirt imbedded in the seams,
dreaming of the last play,
last full swing,
and then my father would walk into the room
with his wool on and...
DAMN ALL WORLDLY POSSESSIONS!!

El Rancho

Hard by the railroad tracks
along Sinsinawa Avenue,
where Misty Black was shot and killed
after her midnight show,
a man shows his face
from the other side of the river.
The new entrepreneurs are young
and have no conscience,
they open arm-wrestling parlors
bust their women up.

When I was 7 years old my mother told me
put on a fresh shirt, wash your face, comb your hair.
We were going to have fried chicken at the El Rancho.
Its walls were covered with animal skins
and the little town was buzzing.

There's a long, spiral road leading down to the bloodstains.
Thick woods cover cracked and dismantled stone steps,
leading to nowhere in particular, in a land
that has no memory, in a country
that tries to hide the Indian treasures
built into its framework.
The river surges like a newborn infant
getting ready to create a ruckus.

The Young Losers

If the same kid rattled your screen door now
you wouldn't know him.
Size or height is not a factor,
but length of vision,
the time it takes for seed to nudge past
the moon's temptress grin
into bright red crescents of tomatoes.

Do not think of myself
as the same kid who leavened the earth
with a few whacks at his basement punching bag,
or scooped up tornadoes
with a clump of grass,
wet, self-embalming fungi
hopping wildly into sex-starved
penetrable darkness,
the trees glowering of cherry, apple, plum.
Roman Catholic marriages,
Roman Catholic ovaries.
It's all the same, a sinful vanishing act
from sublime to indifferent to sublime,
a lonely boy's funeral full of patchwork grace.

Moose

The gift of Maine is the great moose,
but most people like them dead.
While misty mornings hunting grouse
may be good for some,
hunting dumb, harmless moose
is second-to-none.
Rivers wake me up
with their feverish languor,
as if beneath them lurked our own deaths.
Why do they want to kill
the great Maine moose?
It slides by the dark, green mass
of trees and fertility.
Be it dumb, dashed, or defeated
the moose rummages the night
for a moon,
with sad, round eyes
gone wrong.

Visiting Writer

We are grown men,
or at least we're supposed to be.
I think of women
wanting to control the world
through makeup and mothering.
Iowa is a vast incubator.
Several hundred young seminarians
want to touch the smooth-skinned hills,
brown maize, tinted orange.
Here, boys grieve for the lost son.

I think of women who would put on
makeup
for these boys,
and I think of men
who wish to mold them
and make them permanent mothers.

All out there,
over the hills,
on the highway of America.

The Cave

It remains a legendary place,
somewhere below two homes
on a ridge near a hill
though not approximate to anything
within my range of thought,
anchored to a deeply rooted vine
that was my salvation
and led to a short drop to the bottom.
A serenity there, below humanity,
a hidden hole signifying separation
from whatever was bothering us.
The vine hanging free,
the space between it and the other side
a muddy pit, gelatinous,
as our bodies languished there,
dreaming of wooly mammoths.

I see my body in the womb,
the way it was before the world became lunatic,
where order separates time from its frames,
and time bends to the meandering willow.
That space has shrunken all who entered it
into dust particles.
The night tells you to get lost,
stay out of the rain.

Secret Chambers

My mother walks around in her cold, dark house,
never counting years, or weeks, or even minutes.
The mice in her head go round and round,
the furnace walls decay, bats in the attic
stay stuck in funereal silence
(they may or may not be dead,
after years of wailing).
Wings flack against the coils and plaster,
cracked Christmas ornaments and fuses.
Might be offspring of the bat
my father thwarted with a broom
on a night when I covered my head with bedsheets,
not ready for that bat-faced brutal truth.

That's why I like traveling in a car, at night,
with limitless road ahead.
No dirges, no bats,
and you know precisely
when the clouds come by.

Signatures Scribbled on Hotel Stationery

Life is incidental,
except in its reflection of minutiae.
Like the square-foot piece of Alaskan land
my brother has owned for over 40 years,
courtesy of a Wheaties boxtop.
Is it still there, in the place we remember it being?

The strange aura of summer pervades
what is now a wasteland of old women,
detached from their dead, unchanging men.
The scrawled signatures of dead or retired ballplayers
locked away, too important
to be left in the dressing-room drawer.
The large, looped 'd' of Ted Williams
folds into a field of forest green.
The hush of the crowd
that blows by cloud and dust and dream.

Blue Schoolhouse

The intersection of thoughts,
borne out of childhood,
seems just out of reach of reality
and courses through the blood of two boys,
born two generations ago in the middle
of an apathetic land.
They are witnesses, but to what they do not know.
The blue building that flashed by
when I rode on the high school bus
had something in its core
that bothered but fascinated me.

The blue schoolhouse fascinated my brother, too,
independently, without either of us
having knowledge of this integrated thought,
when, 25 years later, the idea emerged as one.
The blue building,
the purple days,
the glass enclosures.
What could it be keeping from us
that so rivets our gaze
there, in the sleepy river town?

Invocation

Brutal things killing harmless things
killing powerful things
killing souls in transit.
The house went dark where the cricket moved
and I, in a chill,
could tell the accuracy of the kill
and the cricket's thick blood
and my intent as I killed it,
blood thickening in the sun and drying,
to be washed into the soil
and born into things that would kill again,
as close to it as if nothing human this could be
but some craving to spill blood
and then, sleeping,
to ravage the rose,
this planet moving toward destruction.
Watch a rose petal fall off and darken,
like blood that's been spilled by the kill,
like beauty too innocent
to remain unbrutalized.

Hybrid

In the car, the angle of your face
electrified hail, falling on the farms
we sped by on Route 20.
We'd lost all our money on the ponies,
you and me, and all those easy bills
were stapled to your brain.
"When I drove Peria," you were thinking
(you couldn't pronounce the 'o')
"there wasn't a mark on the road."
Those fresh scars cut a swath through the land,
unfertile husks of wheat laying lost to the storm.

Doc forbade the hundred proof stuff
that raised the highway to the size of your hand.
Your sallow face sneered at the gods,
as the Impala turned into a truck
filled with bootleg liquor.
The cargo rattled with such force you grimaced.
Only when we reached the familiar lights of town
did you speak again.

Quest

I remember a cold evening in October
when acorns were spilling
spilling
spilled along the grass,
little lost eyes.
I hurried home with my golden leaf,
inserted it into my book,
and hopped the next freight in my dream.
When I awoke I was writing these words,
many years later, unprepared
for what I thought
was another uninterrupted thought.

I recall the short, cylindrical building
where she lived, the red wine and pasta,
perfect for the words I'd just scribbled out
like bruised roses rubbed into stone,
as the sun set in the park across the street.
We hesitated, and in that moment
the light turned red, then green, and red again.

Tonight I tried to take out roots from centuries ago,
pruned under the earth to separate fiber from seed,
but I stopped as the sun went down.
I always manage to feel better when the roots are gone,
when memory distances itself from pain,
the great ballparks live again
and you see yourself alive, a child.

Cashmere

Gone my mother's cashmere sweater,
her last Christmas present,
stolen by someone in the nursing home
after her death.
Gone, her last divination, a dream of sons unborn.
Gone, her vision of the brick house, its two young boys
frolicking in the living room
while a television drama played out.

The cashmere was delicate, like her heart,
and no one can ever know how many times
she wore it. Whoever wears it now
bends into the wind a little differently,
plays out their days
with the knowledge of her frailty and goodness.

There is a little boy on the grass
waiting for his mother to come out on the lawn,
take him to the movie theater,
and there, in the flickering dark,
the outline of her face,
as he wonders what life is like
when hills recede into the past.

Part Two

The City

The city dare not drug you,
see you to the dungeon
white corpuscle alley,
your own bones shining in wine cellars,
a you of animation and neon
casting a finger heavenward
as saints kneel in front of you, begging to be heard.

The city dare not starve you,
it serves best those who eat.
Darlings of the Wall Street faction
bury you with their eyes, their secrets
held by stockbrokers in well-lit office towers.
Hedonists heed the Bible on Sundays,
three wives on Wednesday,
and snicker like dandelions hanging onto air.

The city dare not bite you
for your teeth are sharp and pointy,
your body in a crouch, ready to bolt
with compact dynamite charge and reach for orgasm
in any way possible, with any fantasy,
any soft shade of lipstick or arched heel,
any leg freshly shaved and drenched in Fifth Avenue perfume,
and you have her for one night, come inside her
and depart as quarreling penguins would,
into vast arctic fog.

The city dare not regard you,
for its tramps will have a holiday with crumbs
outside the 21 Club, and the trenches from 42nd to 49th streets
bleed gastric spots.
A man you'll never know spits on your shoe,
the shoeshiner calls you a motherfucker
as he looks upon another man's clean black suit,
the lone scream of a paralyzed woman
comes from a room above your head,
millions of misinformed with open mouths
drink in the violet light.

The city dare not caress you,
for it will make you grotesque,
set you to wonder whether there's a seam in your mind
where an impulse sneaked in,
a warm hand reached for a stranger
to question his hallucinating eyes, directed him
to the right side of the road
and watched him limp off with a distinct twitch
in his right pinky finger, head bowed,
murmuring words his father once spoke that drive him on,
sending him to the boss man for a ride uptown
into the cardboard streets of Harlem
for a first and last fix, a settlement that judges no one,
and even admires his daring, smiles for his daring,
as those words are held tight to his tongue
and he freezes to death.

The city dare not analyze you,
the Hudson and East rivers will never meet,
can never meet.
It is a Herculean thing when cities die,
Barnes and Noble must be able to sell books,
there must be that infinitely sad, obese man
at the head of the diner, taking on the country, secretarial pools,
heads of state, Presidents, Guadalcanal, the MTA,
the rights of females versus males,
abortion, and his wife,
who endlessly supports his gambling habits
so she can endure a night in bed with him,
city that knows all of this is true
and yet reels from any identification
with its values, structure, origin.

The city dare not praise you,
for then the critics come down
with silver words chiseled into huge type casing,
Broadway full of middle-American tourists
who buy the words, adjectives of satisfaction,
and sleep with the knowledge that the treadmill is humming,
and humming well.

The city dare not undermine you,
otherwise you become savage and attack doormen,
drink two six-packs of beer with a dozen poppers,
then start painting your kitchen with sawdust
and the strawberry jelly you've had for a month,
meditating you find a rhythmic sutra, your spine straightens,
you perceive the other side of your body
and bombs exploding in foreign countries.

The city dare not release you
or read your favorite mule quiver that crystallizes action.
Subways smattered with graffiti irk the moneyed and powerful.
Guile motivates kids in New Jersey factory pits,
rebellious infernos of grease dwelling on time and Michelangelo,
to paint the battered cars that come into the yards.

The city dare not catch you
for in its hands you are blind,
a white skeletal uniform hangs from your private ward
where odors of wasted food seep,
a tuning fork resounds in your nightmares,
you steal out the back door
into twilight,
as the city blinks out,
mercifully.

Alone, To New York

One-seventh-of-a-mile indicators
flash on the highway signs
on a muggy day.
I have spent my fingernails
and the stench of Gary, Indiana
is long behind me, though the clouds here
look the same,
and weigh almost as much.

Hart Crane swims somewhere
in the East River.
I beg of myself to hang in
and spin the web I will become.
I am a wild-haired boy
who likes to roam, and wills himself
o'er the plain.
I am goose-eyed and take wrong turns.
I make my heart stop
when I get too close to something I want.

Sounds seem to part the waves in this city, I think.
At George's party I meet the gray cat Cosmo,
many lurching people who don't know me,
a few innocent ones who wish to know
why we live,
a young man who idolizes me
and a bridge that has been crossed
again and again, by wild-haired men like me,
with no sense of time,
with no sense of place.

NYC, October Night

God gored this holy island out,
said some men will be those of crime,
some those of kindness.
A shot of debased southern cross-eyed vengeance
hangs like a sword above the naïve faces.
We get them a little hang-doggish,
too much lipstick on pretty girls who tease
and then leave.
Shy types breeze into town
and level it with their whatever-grins;
we go under to a new beat
rip the old grain apart.
A bum feeds on every heartbeat.
What do we do with a god who knows
he opened up this wound,
cement and all?

Night At the Vanguard

Zoot on alto.
I always come back
to glow with the red curtains
and red walls.
Max is nowhere to be found.
Nirvana is lost in smoke.
I have an advantage, being amusing,
perverted, and dumb.
Zoot in red-striped tie
but it's too purple to tell why.
We fade in and out
of our sex
our sax.
I always come back
to the blood-red curtains,
the blood-red walls.

The Jaded Impresario

In that first instant the city's lights bathe in your dream
like a celestial crown placed on an uncluttered head,
and night is sheathed in aqua and black and a silvery gray,
beneath which the steady thumping of horns and drums
blunt the tones of your face, sending the cryptic messenger
into cries of absolute inconsolable sobbing.

The first time I saw beauty in the ice-blue dawn,
by the bridge trestles when the city was unmasking its horror,
the frantic search for miracle and solemnity
merged in my soul, and filled me with torment so strong
I had to lay down and rest my head,
dead from song.

I took my father's eyecup,
the one he used on selfsame eyes
with a spasmodic flick of wrist,
its concave shape that twisted obliquely out of focus,
and I glorified the eye and what it could do
in a city so selfless and unafraid.
The eyecup washes out all the impurities,
melding like kingfish in the fractious waters of eternity.

Sentiments From a Used Car Lot in Jersey

Over there, on the isle of Paradise,
they have their own fantasies, like driving the soul
out their bodies and not recognizing their faces
in a Bloomingdale's mirrored bathtub.
Now here, we got a different system,
based on the one-to-one theory.
That's a girl for every passion,
and a hot junkheap of chrome and burnished leather
to match any ol' gumdrop's fast foot.
We not only can walk on water,
we can drive on it, and murder with our eyes,
and just before depositing our fenders on West Street,
we jump out and flash that familiar S-M-I-L-E
that makes loblips out of satin queens
and dry, Satanic men into holy rollers.
Dont'cha read the papers, fire has no name,
and please don't beg your mothers
to send you home again.
There's a battered coupe in Jersey City
pointed straight at that great gorge.
What an unfeeling Paradise!

The Monk Is Dead

When I could not stand to look
at that white pillar
in the middle of my living room
in the East Village
I fought off a blizzard wind and stinging rain
to get to a Monk album:
pianissimo erotica.
In his coma he must have played
every note again,
and smiled through his decaying brain
that all was dead.
That damn rain will slash you
when you least expect it.

Pigeons of 50th St.

The vagrants have gone away
or stayed awake, sweating.
A woman stands, dazed
for the hell of it.
Through a breaking sky
paths of blue and Swiftian clouds
full of embrace.

On Saturday mornings
I tutor two young men
who wait for the words
as we all do, as willingly
as pigeons fly through cut glass
and crumple at our feet, to die.

The red tenements
shiver like new paint
and above them the endless
hungry and searching faces
mirrored in our eyes.
The fat cats do not believe
in simple trust.
That is what makes reality upsetting.

Today, Nate will not be there
to be tutored.
He will have gone back to Lenox Avenue,
grabbing the first dealer to come along
his wife and child in the balance.

And pigeons who will themselves to die
fluttter inside a celestial kingdom.

Sunrise

Sleep tries to reason with us,
but it does not stay us.
She moved under her pillow,
reticent to acknowledge the dream
as it wove beyond my sight.
The sun cackled like Van Gogh's burning fields,
and I recall how I contemplated the tattered clouds
holding up my youth.

I have much to do.
I will leave her until we complete the answers.
But I cannot do more than walk,
scan the anonymous buildings.
Gore the light from a sunflower.

City Girl

I watch her change every Friday night,
the mannequin in the window at Saks.
Sometimes she greets me from a divan,
sometimes she asks too much of me,
sometimes she doesn't even wink
sometimes she is so glamorous she refuses
to believe her heartlessness.

I watch her from behind the windshield
and she seems to forgive me
for all the bad things I've done,
for how I can turn on people,
the cruelty
when I'm away from her.
It's a talent I have for saying the wrong thing.
But she doesn't care.
She'll be home before morning,
and if it's raining I don't have to wait up.

Ethel

Ethel Merman followed me home one night
in my dream, a miserable, besotted night,
and asked me if she could type my novel.
She was trying to make a buck as a stenographer
on Skillman Avenue, and I said to her:
"You were a great singer, and I read your obituary."
She laughed and said she had to get her hair done
because Broadway producers liked gals
who were primped, and I smiled and scanned the sky
as it continued to cascade rain, and said,
"Okay, I'll give you my novel to type,
but make sure you stay within the margins."
She said: "Sure, Sonny, I'm real speedy."
And I began to think that someday
she would sing at the top of her lungs
in front on an SRO crowd at The Palace,
and she wants to type some words
so she can get more chewing gum
and her hair fixed.

When I unlocked my door
I decided I wouldn't call her.
I'd let her become famous by herself,
even if she did have to type someone else's book.

Bread

Typing on my knees,
the last pose of an idiot-savant
or someone who might relish
hand-to-hand combat with the masses.
Upon the stage I kneel,
head bent to the light,
imagining
the Brooklyn Bridge
cars passing into the night
along its threadbare legacy.
Bodies fished out of the East River,
the men who sold your father's father
bread.

Mantle

He swung hard
his muscles a wave
extending along the rich apartments
of the Bronx,
throbbing with the beat of the city.
Balls disappeared into bleached shirts
like falling stars.
Eisenhower was showing us the good life.
It was going going gone,
oh so gone.

Behind the pillars of the old Yankee Stadium,
hands reaching as one for the white missile.
Reach, reach,
for it is gone.

Flight Plan

Blue-jet pulse light coming from LaGuardia,
from its mottled haze of fume
above frantic humanity, the unnecessary
baggage
      of lives
      & I am encouraged to sing
unencumbered by this thing
      called Future
      or books from these skyways
planning our layaway deals
      & drowning sorrows in pills
      & methane.

Grand judger, if you could signal
from your tower
      some faith
      to swallow   with water
      with water
what would it be
      and where would we land?

Tentative

The orbs that make up my eyes
are exposed thin, blood platelets
that want to explode.
Instead they squint at the sun,
bad lighting, and the dead.
The dead are precious only because they are few.
Check the newspaper for references.
A boy goes out to collect money for school
and is killed by a teenager
who would do anything for love.

Now there comes a time when I must leave,
put on a suit that conforms to time and space,
put on.
Now there is a time for regret, and long distances
between friends and familiar scenes.
Eventually the reflections are lost in a shroud,
a very warm day in autumn,
a hard rain,
a blowing snow.
That is why I hold my daughter close to my heart,
to hear the other heart working
to hear her sing to me,
her sweet lips giving me a goodnight kiss
and the emptiness of space whirling around me.
Until I wake up in the middle of my coffee,
checking for references.

The Plot of the Maidens

The maidens are coming for me tonight,
on this nondescript street where hooded figures tramp past,
and the past is looking west
toward rolling hills of midnight green.
It matters not what kind of night transpires,
full of snow and swirling ice,
or quiet, summer mild,
the century plays out with the outcasts of time
who have interbred, ingested far too many chemicals,
who meet the newcomers in U.S.-certified denim,
who know not one bit of history of the country
they so gallantly stride through.

All the landmarks you knew
that riveted your childhood memories
are rusted iron and museum gray.
The house I grew up in is cold,
my mother bent over in mumbling solitude
in a place she can't call home.
Earth, its core boiling yet its outside numb.
My old bedroom full of unwanted pennants,
spider-webbed and doomed.

They don't know where I am,
but the maidens are relentless.
They want my entrails and brain,
the soft parts of my palate.
So I prefer to stay here, in the battlements of this house,
where I can keep an eye on everything,
every sinister face, every errant sound.
The maidens know that night passes rapidly.
In the morning, their faces will be knotted in the tree roots
that grow into the sewer.

July In The Fundamental City

I run out of brain,
which rests here in the muggy midnight
with the radio on like a primal beast,
in the shadows of bullets
ripping into babies' stomachs.
The voices on talk radio riot on
about society run amok, girls raped for fun,
fun being her frozen smile on the police blotter.
Too many arguments about money and logic
killed his freedom.
Pillared gray buildings grip the vortex of the city,
surround the legs of commerce.
Talk turns to the kingmaker deal,
the one he'll do to buy his Westchester house
when it comes down.
Here we are, say the lions of 42nd Street,
here is the terror of palsied hands.

When the Roar of Uptown Meets Downtown

When the heavy apparatus thunders by
and you've been raped by one eye,
who notices?
Sardine trampolines wind like caterpillars
past iron stakes
that hold the city in its sanctum.
Out from underneath,
the last of us groan and grimace,
and shake off thousands of hands
that have been on us.
But when the express lanes meet
all masses retreat,
for the blur is a whir
and the enemy
within.

Tabula Rasa

Tonight I look at my ties
and I never want to wear one again.
I never want to lose an eye.
I rub the orbs
around and around the epithelium.
It is this intense blue, these snake eyes
that take me into my bloodstream.
It was that first night
with a little too much booze,
the fissure in the sky where stars begged our pleasure
and the unknown woman howled in laughter,
sexy but not wanting to show too much of it.

Tonight I look up at my ties
and I never want to be in them again.
Manufactured style is no style at all.
My father never bought custom-designed anything,
why should I?
My father's polka-dotted ties
hang like carcasses in vultureland.
Then there was the night he was fitting his shoe
and the shoehorn flew out of his hand
behind a curtain,
and we never found it
because we decided to stop looking.

Opening

A new film opens this week at the Waverly,
young crowd, dangerous looks that are really quite tame.
Animals looking for a watering hole,
blondes dished up like paradise
ink in their hairdos,
muscular boys back from a workout,
wondering if they'll continue to wonder—
Sixth Avenue trade
Crazy Eddie timebomb,
a primordial sound mix.

It doesn't matter what the actors say,
except for the occasional esthete
who jots things down
and twitches in his seat.
The actress is any man's fantasy,
she will recite any stray lines.

Evolution

There will be murder,
there will be the lovely way
she shatters eggs with her mouth.
There will be thunder,
and the immaculate breadth
of her bosom.

There will be libraries for the blind
and cages for the passive.
Disease will never offend us,
the ugly will rule.
Once people have all they can possibly desire,
the milkmaid will ring your doorbell
and do that dance she promised you
when she was 18, and ravishing.

An Evening With Mother Marishka

On Bleecker Street, an Asiatic cathedral.
I've come in here for my future
but the palm reader's dark-haired daughter in pearl
longs to be touched by foreign hand.
The moon strangles me, mother feels it,
the lines on my palm cracking
and dispersing at the top.
Chakra fire rising!

But your child, mother!
Goddess of a long-ago-erotic-turn-of-flesh.
A ferocious kiss never mounted.
Mother, if I want her in my dreams
I will remember the coming of her womanhood.
Mother, she is your dove,
you, her willow tree.
Do not consider what I am
but what she will be.

Honeymooning

While we danced between thunderclaps
and stole for the Paris Opera House doors,
trembling fingers felt for the crevices of dusty mirrors.
For a long while I could not find you,
and my father called out my name
as "Gloria in Excelsis Deo"
filtered over me from the balcony.
I knew he was succumbing to the pain,
his brain a mollusk, receding.
At the colonnade we faced the rain,
heard a false cue from the orchestra pit.
Death peeled far off in recesses of sky
that separated us from our dreams.

Contemplating New York, Again

The urban world is unhappy.
I can feel its bent muscles,
ideas melting at the surface.

The portable heater is on
and I write on my lap, with no cachet, no title,
some fractured light throwing me off.
I'm mad at what happened to me,
here in a desolate place of my own choosing.
I'm mad because my father mocked my writing
in the hot June of my last Illinois summer,
the river over the horizon lost
in a slow hydraulic mystery.

The urban world is full of lost porcelain figurines,
my father among them,
porcelain terrified into odd shapes
concealed by glass-shadowed sepulchers.

The knife is the city, and I its hand.

Pulse

You finger your horn.
You finger your life.

You finger your horn,
all down the line your life.

You finger it alone,
your life.

You finger brass
sweat down the horn.

You finger your brassy horn,
sweat out your life.

You sweat on your mouthpiece,
hold in your horn.

You eat gold tongue-pieces,
body your horn.

You finger the airholes
of your horn, your lifeblow.

You finger your skillet brow
horn of your life.

You finger this thing,
the horn, this thing.

Obituary

The dead clarinetist danced with his instrument
upon wet cement in New York; the lights refracted
a partial drop of blood where he lay,
Jimmy Condon in his dreams.
His face was abused from notes that had altered the moon,
his hip jutting to an unusual object in space
an alternative form of eye
that we would be able to pick from a photograph
if we were used to it.

I bless that part of us which is never untrue,
which disguises the tenuous hold we have on life,
which unveils tears as they blend in with our bone.
When we are unloved we are like the dead clarinetist,
a little stain imbedded in the sidewalk
that we walk on with our shoe polish
until it doesn't even grin anymore.

Kulture

O'Hara wrote about that smoke
coming out of the Camel man's mouth
in the 50s gray-edge dawn of Times Square
where he puffed in his regulated room
in the district of mad-legged lovers.

Walking squeamish, the people
who wanted to blurt out
"Squeeze me, nudge me,"
that, my friends, was the start of the cold shoulder.
Why do you think we had 35 years
of cold war?
We don't want it to get hot,
cause we'll all be gone
and gone is not cool,
it's better to stay alive
to drown in propaganda
forever cold
welcome to the cold war
again, brothers.

The giant billboard of the cigarette pack,
the smart skirts of genteel city folk
must have made O'Hara want to creep back
to his regulated room to seek shelter
from the rise of glass on glass
mirror on mirror.
Today we read about the Red Menace
just south of Florida,
we can't see the individual
don't take time to notice him,
and O'Hara's room with his hairbrush and Camels
is left to other men, other pastimes.

The Trapped Negro

The trapped negro
ran toward Mama Bones –
one leg out of the cab,
one mouth cursing.
I followed closely
heart to rib,
till Eighth Avenue
where screams were veiled
by smoke
from a manhole cover.
I had eyes in my pockets,
tongue in my nose.
A bead of sweat stung my forehead.
The wind blew it into dust
on the way home.

Analysis of Earth

Beneath compost heaven,
in the paradox of god and antihero,
lies a man.
This is his hemoglobic pipeline,
the tattered clouds.
This is his mouth-dripping awe,
a picture postcard of New York City
bought
when he was freckles and blotches
(a lack of white chromosomes).
Here lies a man.
Bridges make his feast.

Last Night Together, West Side

It was only George and that crutch,
a gnarly white-toothed construction,
and he was using it to aim for the 8-ball, side pocket
while the regulars inched the stools back
at The Donegal.
And the carom was good,
the crutchless old man laughed
showed one black tooth,
a pedestrian came in to see what the holler was about,
and we tipped brandies
from the last two bottles in the house.

Maybe one fist was thrown,
maybe one person got away
without getting rained-on,
but the car was gassed for Mexico
and one sad girl went home to Long Island
guessing who her next lover would be.

The Streets

In the language of the gods
we are all feeble enemies
who live in bodies we have every reason to hate.
We do not pass each other
as if we were in this together, as if
we had something inside us
that was or would be
equally satisfying for someone else
to have.
And we hate because we see those gods
imploring us to become as powerful
as we can, with murder and malice outlawed
but acceptable and accepted.
We laugh in the company of others
at parties of self-congratulation
and we earn what we can to become part
of a fabric called the human environment.
Can we really love ourselves
without giving witness to others,
who never would allow us to feel this way
if we did not gather, eyeball to eyeball,
for some kind of response,
however meaningless?

Poem

I have a power for words
they couldn't understand.

They're all dead in the throat,
swallowed up in yellow newsprint.

The Catholic dream is you're here to serve,
and any false act of the tongue is evil.

But then you sense a convulsing cry,
the hollow tone of a dying man's curse.

He had summarized his life in two words,
and the priest added five.

A desire for sameness will lead us to the altar,
but never to salvation, never to our hearts.

All the young form an array of irregulars
content on staying with the formula.

And me?
I'll sit on a crag with Ezra Pound,
black coffee, ocean, and a maddening roar.

Tour of Manhattan

The great facades fade
into the channels of the Midwest
like some unorthodox calling of forces,
pigeon droppings in wet snow,
patrons of the flesh
flesh no more.

Cathedrals are stone lummoxes.
Nigerians peddle gold in front of Bloomingdale's.
An ill wind blows in front of an old lady's face,
she slaps it away.
Paper whirls into noon, the mechanics are dead.
No cries can be heard from the great facades,
only the neverending cascade of chalices.

Torment

A sculptor screamed "I love you!"
from a passing bus
to a woman
in Paris.
She undressed in his rented atelier.
He wrought her thighs,
her Elizabethan neck.
She became gaudy stone, indelicate.

"Your life is not stable," she said,
undressing in front of him for the last time.
In a freezing Brooklyn apartment,
a bust of red clay frowns into a naked lightbulb.
He bears the weight of her face
in his unfinished beer.

Sitting In the Lever House Building, 1987

It is a perfect 70-degree day and no one cares.
This day, like so many others, was created for postcards.
No more bustling magic here,
no women out for an after-lunch stroll down Madison Avenue,
the type of woman who might kiss you one day
on some strange brownstone step.

Along the wall are aligned the soaps, detergents,
cleansing agents of a 1950s kitchen.
Snapped out of a dream and an era, I walk outside,
a poet in a suit and tie ready to scream.

When future archaeologists take apart New York City,
they'll start here, with the straight lines, rectangular halls,
the dead energy.
Eternally shielded from the sun
and nursing large boils,
the citizenry will put on their best faces.

Training Models

They keep them on non-allergic foods
and a maximum of 10 calories a day,
they feed them beautiful Swedish virgins
out of prep school,
they dance them with non-threatening lights
where their pores can open up,
they bathe them in ultraviolet
and pack them to Bermuda,
they hold them on a string to powerful ad men,
who sign their college degrees
put them on the cover of Seventeen
and keep them on contract till they're 21.
They make lots of money, take a little drug,
do a little kink, front a little stuff,
and give boring interviews
when they're 30, pregnant,
and their lives are just beginning.

The Dissolution

The gloss of the young girl's lipstick
matches the color of fashion mavens' dresses
(who slash at the cuffs of their pants
as they bow to the whims of their masters.)
Even now, as the moon passes over this realm
of madness and fake congeniality,
we brace ourselves
for what's beyond our children's lives.

Tourists eye the ornamentation on buildings
like fish wrapped in newsprint,
newsprint hyping a 1961 debutante ball at the Waldorf.

Spaces

Evil comes quickly.
Motors deadened by the weight of all they carry,
and the damp air of January,
signal a return to the obvious human things:
what eyes we choose,
what order we would put to things
we cannot order.
Doesn't it seem like these buildings
are fortifications for dreams
that rouse us
that crush our bones
with the concrete shadows bearing down on us?

In the trains, buses, and subways,
throughout the nexus of blood,
we are embryos.
Nothing to haunt us but ourselves
and the motors we run with
when the city's lights burn the black dawn.

Nights Gone By

The supermarket across the street
with its neo-Roman architecture
was once a moviehouse showing hushed crowds
the peak of Gregory Peck's nose.
We are each bent toward the other's attachment,
the next spoken word.
When we discover a wound
it recovers and appears as a still frame.

There are no more lines,
and the can-and-bottle Deposit Center
stands where the ticket-booth lady said "Hello."
Tears and credits marching as one across the screen
drown out this cold night.
Reduced to caricatures,
a man in tweed, a woman in velvet.

To all of you who were there,
who became the spaces
where flickers of knowledge danced up
and out of the theater,
know that the dragons of the Chrysler Building
are coming off their perches,
looking for something to eat.

Mass Murderer

Driving through the amplified Midwest
a rented car my only companion
while a madman kills all he can
and the calmest, palest voices describe the rampage.
We are not pretty when dissecting mayhem.
I'm behind glass and air-conditioning,
but out there are lives of edginess and hatred.
It seems I am framed here,
a bit of the wilderness,
privy to the workings of a mass murderer.

I take a room in Youngstown, Ohio,
stumble to the shower,
shake off the shakes.
Then I go down to the bar around midnight
and watch "Death Wish III" with three strangers.
Everyone's friendly, everyone's looking for a sign
in the other's eyes.
There's something so human here is defies explanation.
Some answers come silently out of the wilderness.

Walking Past Woolworth's, After the War

There we are, strains of each other,
the long, loping stride,
there is my father, ahead of the pack.
Could be 42nd Street, could be downtown,
his uniform on, home from the war
while a sturdy brunette picks up her step
behind him.
But she is well behind him,
somewhat in awe of him.
That's all you can see in the photograph:
the Woolworth sign, my father, the brunette,
and some serious faces fading into the background.
Voices are pushing him into his 40s,
spurring him on, just as I am by an energy,
unidentifiable.
There is much that remains hidden in a chemical reproduction,
yet we do not question any part of it.

In the concrete canyons I'm left with memories
of that swagger, that youth,
a snapshot that maps the earth
with unwritten pains.

Dream In Red Dusk

Dream: gathered around are well-dressed people
with drinks in their hands, in an ornate place
open to the sun, maybe Italy.
A red ball, plastic, irregularly shaped,
rolls to a halt across from a suspicious-looking man.
I have had too many martinis and need a nap.
I go to my hotel room
wake up to news of an explosion.
There are 18 dead, including my brother.

Reality: moving across the edge of Queens, N.Y.,
counting the water towers, integrating the soot and grime,
trying to come up with various endgames,
who will be saved and how,
while porticos of lost worlds open to nowhere.

All wisdom must fail,
all rhythms must wane,
all of us must look into each other's eyes,
if only for seconds.
I go back to the site of the explosion,
the guard lets me in.
I try to find the center of the blast,
the place where I saw the red ball.
Was it there?
Did someone remove it to displease me?
Why couldn't I save him? Everyone?
No matter what the philosophers tell you
never try to remember your birth.

For me it was quite simple:
first I saw sky, then I shouted,
shout of joy, I languished on the floor,
then something red grew in the trees
(which to me was the reason for being),
the reason I kept searching all those long winters,
the reason I've been gone 20 years now,
the room as I recall it, a sofa hard and unyielding.

Laying There

Time is threadbare.
A break in the weather.
New York is a set of mesmerizing eyes
in a goldfish bowl.

They sliced you gill to gill
to get at a vermin cell,
and now your cute pudginess
submits to lumps, bruises, scars, and crayon lines.
You try to rise from bed but you can't push it.

I hear you breathe.
I hear you as I put on my t-shirt, brush my teeth,
drink a beer.
I am a thousand miles away, beering my belly,
only to watch it fade, form, and fade.
I am a part of the Old West, as you were.
I remember that grainy photograph of you
in Pennsylvania Station.
True as highway ribbons and death,
true as my seedling eyes bear red lines
of sleeplessness and drink,
there is love across the chasm.

Christmas Eve, 1981

Every year I make peace with my father
in the form of an unanswered prayer,
from a pigeon coop on a tenement building
in the Bronx,
in the smashed window with spray paint,
from the image of his humpty-dumpty frame
outside the bus depot,
rain of rusty nails a camouflage
for the purity of our kiss.

Every instant of his life
reveals itself in his vacant eyes,
the amber sunsets over Manhattan,
the ghost flight of one of his liquor trucks,
as he earned money with the finesse he knew he had,
America about him dying in the throes of war and depression.

Every midnight he inches to the kitchen
for bologna on rye,
and every Christmas he takes his fate in stride,
as the neighborhood milk truck
pulls out of the alleyway, and briefly,
seems lost on the road whence it came.

A Telephone Call Made In An Attempt to Stir Communication

Over the dumb, sweet miles
I try to save a friend, I try to have this woman-friend
give him a call with no strings attached
because somehow I find us all searching blindly
for a movement, a peep out of the show
of life, like we're all dumb mules
looking for directions to the sun.

The night broods in that Midwest laconic sadness
especially at 20 below zero,
and nothing vegetable survives.
I am an incomplete power in the universe too,
as much in need of help as he is,
and yet, here I am, the psychiatrist,
calling the woman who once had that secret power
in her eyes for me, to raise him from lethargy.
It can never happen.

I know all the places where the rails splint.
She says she'll try to say hello to him
when he walks his regular beat, by the library.
I realize there is no communication that's fit for him.
I should have known fifteen years ago,
when he started to go off.
All those highways and sky,
and what do we have but a greater love gone yearning
in the cold void of people who can't get involved
because of all the becauses,
and the strange people who walk alone.

Wife

You are as you were to me
many years ago, which you may not believe.
The smile is the same beautiful, sexy loop,
the eyes have the same mystique,
trying to find the goodness in everyone.
Time has taken its toll on both of us,
has disturbed our sense of self.

I have not told you how much you do for me
and how I love you for giving us our daughter,
and how that is good enough for now,
but perhaps I should.
For she has taken your beauty and made it her own,
only disguised it with your giving heart,
two beating as one inside me.

Gruesome Morning

Laundry lay crippled on the floor,
my head gearing up for a new job,
my daughter asleep in her whorl of demons
and the night lying ragged along the coasts of time.
Was I arrogant to think that I could change
the color of forests, the hue of camouflage,
the ambivalence of millions?
I just want to play with my cowboy and Indian figures
in a mud puddle along the Mississippi,
with some intruder on the railroad tracks
eyeing the little boy's crude playthings.

That's what you're born from,
the mire of simple things,
the ugly plastic of foreign factories,
the gestating wings of seagulls
in the air above the bay.
What do I care if I die with my soul
flying into the ripple of the beyond,
a gangster in flight?
My life on earth this child,
asleep in her pristine beauty, denying fate.

Old Cat

There's an honor to being an old cat,
approaching 20 cat years,
for now there is only a vagrant scratch
and a silent moan,
the desires that made you stalk
just memories of conquests.

A slice of sun to sit in, a cool night,
the smell of salmon,
and the knowledge that the world
will someday purge itself of all that poisons it.
My daughter wants a kitten already,
planning for the old cat's death.

I see myself sometimes in the old cat,
the bones a little weaker, the trek to bed a little slower.
Trying to be something of value in this world
is simply asking too much of a human soul,
too much pressure to bear
for someone who merely wants to know
he tried to do the best he could.
And one day he had his claws removed,
but still he whipped them all.

Ninety

Amid a swirling vortex of tongues I search for you,
but you only return an echo of pebbles upon stone.
You emerge in the mirrors you walked by,
disfiguring the blue-black darkness
a noble mask, unguarded.
I hear a cry.
It could be any cry from any street,
but the timbre is different.
I sip my coffee and sit in relative peace,
not the man or boy you knew, nor the one I knew
when you stumbled upon the fox in the alleyway.

Wayward we search, trying to grasp
the essence of 90 years,
which you would have turned today,
the engines, trains, banks, unions,
baseball leagues, theaters, expositions,
all the organized chaos of an emerging nation.

Half-mad, half-saint, you tried to grip the edge
of the mahogany bar,
the palm of your hand feeling for the grit.
As I sit here I ask no more questions,
for the things you and I wanted are similar.
I used to see it as you handed me a cold Pepsi,
my face flushed with the promise
of roads and journeys.

Vanished

There is my life,
vanished.
Slipped like sewing thread
through an eyelet,
vanished.
Skipped out of sight,
mesmerized by the night.
Caromed off the wall,
cannibalized at the policeman's ball,
vanished.

Somewhere last night
I was in my tuxedo,
having the time of my very short life.
There was a woman at the piano.
She signaled for me
to come hear her swing,
listen for her vast knowledge,
and then,
I vanished.

Come look for me sometime,
you won't believe
what this life is like.

Revision

The platform was wooden, tilting,
the crisp autumn air forebode rain
that would send the sensible people home.
My father was coming to hear me read my works,
in a strange cold room, an event I never thought could occur.
And yet, he came into the gathering, visibly fading
from his illness, like a 40-year-old bottle of wine
gestating in a grotesque man's mind.

My derelict ramblings had moved him to think
about how he should respond.
But he could not for his voice cords were frayed.
When he got up to leave a pride filled me,
and in the steady rain he got into the car and drove off,
a young lady watching the horror and confusion in my eyes.

What she didn't know was that I had just glimpsed
the shroud of myself passing away,
and a world was presented to me neither tethered to the earth
nor swirling in space,
but forming an image of death on the blood-splattered stage
where my lungs hung from the microphone stand,
and shuddered.

Perception

The morning fills with light
from the eyes of my daughter.
Winter scorns its critics, and man assaults machine again
like a slow mantra into hell.
I've seen it all before, the pauper of familiar lines
trying to catch up to his lineage.
Is it King Wenceslas, gorging on life,
building his castles, out for a stroll?
Stroll, the translation on my coat-of-arms,
my actual name.

It is 18 years ago, I think of father at home,
his gaze into nothingness as I arrived from my job in New York.
The contrast horrifies.
The appeasement of a slow drink would have been better
than a frenzied search for meaning
over a hurriedly eaten meal.

Upon his death men gathered to reminisce
about his punctuality, his demeanor.
Who would lock up the bar now,
who would carry on those dreamworlds inside his head?
Who would stroll along Charles Bridge,
beneath the Clock of the Apostles,
and turn back time?

Concrete and Dust

In the harrowing drama in my mind,
where the steps I took 20 years ago are gone,
where the men I saw 20 years ago are dead,
and where the girls, reflected in department store windows
are leggy fantasies,
there is my city.

A bemusement, an aroma from the Horn & Hardart
where Daily News scribes went to relive their scoops
among the corned beef sandwiches and coconut cream pies,
now replaced by silent witnesses,
and in their hurry to get into the hotels
are dwarfed by steel, noise, and harlots.
Remove me from the hordes and I simply wish to fill my lungs
with century-old grime and hosiery fossilized in tar,
the indistinct cadences of gone-again, here-again
where no one moves to action
except to counter an elemental reaction.

There goes my city,
trampling my heart, hoping against hope,
trying to stave off annihilation.
Take a deep breath, faint-hearted ones,
for that man reaching for the BLT with fedora in hand
has made of you a foreteller of his dreams,
a god walking among the raggedy mists of time.

Prayer For Tonight

Goodnight and God bless
you strange man known as The Czech,
the man who gets a funny look
or looks like he's a wreck.
It's true, I tend to look away from the masses,
the urban swell, the ones played out.
I gathered it all inside the punching bag
in the dank basement of my home,
pounding at my fears of socializing
while voices talked in hushed tones.
I dreamed I was Marciano, hammering away
at nothing, nothing being clear,
and sobbing as the dust clogged my throat.
I sat down and ran my Lionel trains,
or put some quarters in the rusted slot machines,
envisioning voluptuous beauties surrounding me.

But then I got up and left, a wonderboy in flight.
"That boy's crazy," they said. "He's not right."
Now I ponder my animated beginnings,
the pure boisterous fury that flashed out of sight.
I raced down Seventh Avenue,
had friends believing pedestrians were bowling pins.
Half my life in the country, half in the city,
half my father's age tonight,
who would have had his cake vanilla-creamy
but who bows down at the altar of good
that is his new life.

Goodnight and God bless
(with apologies to Red on the diode tube
that flickers in your wet dreams),
Goodnight and God bless
(you dumb redheaded goddess of pulp),
Goodnight Mother,
you gracious creature of high dreams.

End of the Road

All of your faintest hopes went down with The Crash,
the creatures prodding you to get off the subway,
the newly minted green and pungent cedar,
glorious with the righteous cigar
on Maiden Lane, by the ghost of Alexander Hamilton.

The ships carry our dreams, they carry our feathery weights
in the middle of a tumbling cosmos,
with citizens sure of their wisdom
sure that the apes are not part of men, that man is not part
of what they desire, the hard faces and round voices
of the weary who came to Ellis Island,
their clothes once absorbed by their skin,
which even now floats toward us inside diaphanous petals
spinning pollen into the air.

Hard by the terminal, by the birthplace of commerce,
emerges a hybrid of animal and infant, mentality and brutality,
lie the bones of ragged slaves who touched shore,
lay ashes of the city in a galvanized urn.
The night cools down in flotillas of fame
as water stretches around the harbor
and angels pass out in the catacombs of Exchange Place.
The Federalist Papers swirl out into the land,
West to the Appalachians, toward the Great Lakes,
and over the Mississippi,
where dust collects on the photograph
you forgot to take with you.

Printed in the United States
17142LVS00001B/79-192